AMAZING
INVENTIONS AND CONCOCTIONS

HOWARD ELSON
ILLUSTRATED BY KIM BLUNDELL

D0307844

OCTOPUS BOOKS

Introduction

Did you know that an old biscuit tin played a large part in the development of the television? Or that you can now make a telephone call from a public call-box on board an aircraft in mid-flight? Or that a woman from London, England, devised a chocolate spoon to help children take horrible medicine?

These are just a handful of amazing inventions and concoctions that have been created throughout history. People have always been inventors and ever since pre-historic times, they have been looking for ways to improve the quality of life.

This book features over 160 such innovations and the men and women who made them possible. There are inventions that changed the course of history like radar and the X-ray; some that improved our means of travel like the bullet train and the hovercraft, others that we take for granted in these days of high technology, like the washing machine and pop-up toaster . . .

. . . and others that simply didn't work, like the car that was powered by a gigantic elastic band, or the first pair of roller skates.

Find out for yourself. You'll be amazed!

A Name To Write With

The ball-point pen, which contains quick-drying ink that flows on to a moving steel ball, was patented in 1938 by a Hungarian called Laslo Biro. Had his name been Eric, we would now all be writing letters with an . . . Eric.

Open Wide

I hate going to the dentist.'
How many times have you heard that?

The poor dentist has an awesome reputation — and his or her drill is probably one of the most feared of all medical instruments. Dentists' drills were driven by pedals before they were adapted for use with electricity. George Washington's dentist, John Greenwood, devised the first foot-powered drill by adapting his mother's spinning-wheel. However, the first motor-driven device came from an Englishman called George Harrington in 1863 with the introduction of his hand-held clockwork drill. It probably still hurt as much then as it does today.

Understanding Merlin

Legend has it that Merlin was the wise old magician at the court of King Arthur and the knights of the Round Table, many hundreds of years ago.

Today, however, Merlin is the name of a brand new micro computer that will revolutionise communications throughout the world.

British Telecom have invented a way of translating English into a wide selection of foreign languages over the telephone. It means that a person in England will be able to dial a number anywhere in the world, and through an instrument called a 'translatorphone', she will be understood at the other end of the line, even though she is speaking in English.

Merlin has been programmed to recognise and understand over 400 commonly used English phrases, and translate them, at the touch of a button, into a chosen language. The message is then sent to a foreign telephone where a computer synthesised voice relays the translated words.

Talk to the Animals

Scottish scientist, James Clerk Maxwell, who discovered the existence of electromagnetic waves, used to try out his complicated theories on his dog, Tobi. He regularly held long conversations with the animal, though it isn't known if the dog ever answered back!

A Language Invented By Children

Towards the end of the last century, sugar was a new and booming business in Hawaii. To help with the sudden, thriving industry, many thousands of immigrants were taken to the island from Spain, Portugal, China, Japan, Hong Kong, Korea and other Asian countries. The trouble was, they couldn't understand each other. So communication amongst nations was difficult. They couldn't speak a common language like English or the native Hawaii tongue. It was left to the children of the new arrivals, playing together, to invent a new language of their own, which was known as Hawaiian Creole, and contained words from all the immigrant languages. They then taught their parents!

Superloo

The Automatic Public Convenience – APC – was designed by the French in the 1980s. Operated by a computer, it is a lavatory that automatically cleans itself. After use, the lavatory bowl and floor tip up and are scrubbed by a high speed rotating brush, using pressurised water and disinfectant. The lavatory is then dried by a hot-air jet, and locked back into position. Jets spread deodorant around the small compartment, while piped music is played constantly. The toilet door locks automatically, but unlocks again if the compartment has been engaged for more than 15 minutes.

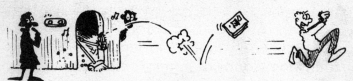

If Music Be The Food . . .

The world's first edible record was made in 1903 by a German company called Gebruder Stollwerck. Flat discs of chocolate were covered with pieces of tin foil, which had grooves etched into their surface, and actually played tunes once they came into contact with a gramophone needle. When the record was finished, it could be disposed of by being eaten.

A Phone Box In The Sky—

You can now phone anywhere in the world from a public telephone system, *even* on board aircraft in the middle of a trans-Atlantic flight. Operated by credit card, the special experimental plane phones have been in use in a dozen different airlines in America since 1983, allowing passengers to make their calls at any time during a flight, apart from take off and landing.

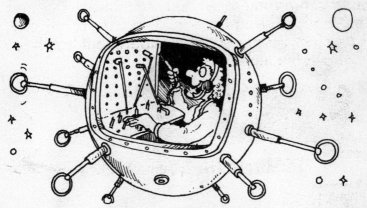

A signal is sent from the telphone instrument via the plane's transmitter and then bounced off an orbiting satellite to a receiving dish in the country to which the call is bound. It takes only a few seconds to get through.

The British prototype system, Skyphone, went into operation in 1988.

A Bumpy Ride

When the first escalator was installed in London, England, at the Earl's Court Underground in 1911, a man called Harris was employed by the station simply to spend his days riding up and down on the moving staircase. Harris, known as 'Bumper', had a wooden leg, and it was thought that his actions would give the public confidence in the new device, if they could see how safe it was.

The escalator itself, using a conveyor belt to pull folding steps up a long slope, was invented by an American called Reno in 1894.

Wish You Were Here

One of the first things you do when you go on holiday is send a postcard to your friends and relatives back home. But have you ever wondered where this idea came from? The man who printed and manufactured the first picture postcard in 1865 was an Italian stationer. called Cesare Bertana. It contained a view of Lake Garda in Italy.

A Three-Wheeled Horse

The tractor was invented to replace horses on farms, and at first, large, mechanical machines driven by steam power were introduced for ploughing. However, it wasn't until 1902 that the first petrol-driven tractor saw the light of day. It was called the 'Ivel Tractor', and was designed by Dan Albone, from Biggleswade, England. It was constructed with three wheels instead of four – two large ones at the back on either side, and a smaller central one at the front. The tyres themselves were made completely out of steel.

Henry Ford made the first mass-produced tractors in 1916.

Ups And Downs

The telescopic umbrella was invented by a German called Hans Haupt in 1930.

The Jet Set

The jet engine transformed aviation history and allowed people to travel at supersonic speeds.

It was created simultaneously by two people working independently of each other – Hans-Joachim von Ohain in Germany, and Britain's Frank Whittle.

Whittle had already designed the first jet engine in the early 1930's. He realised that if planes were to fly at very fast speeds, they would have to fly a lot higher, so that the thinner air at altitude would create less resistance. However, the Royal Air Force turned him down and rejected his theories. 'It is definitely *not practical*,' said an official.

In Germany, meanwhile, the first jet designed by von Ohain, the Heinkel HE 178, made its maiden flight on 27 August, 1939, reaching over 650 kilometres an hour (400 mph). Whittle had to wait for two years until his own Gloster E28/29 took to the air on 14 May, 1941.

The jet works on the principle that air is sucked into the front of the engine and burns with a fuel to form a gas. At high altitudes, the air has to be compressed before it reaches the engine – Frank Whittle overcame this problem by using a gas turbine engine to compress the air. Hot gases from the turbine are then forced out through a jet pipe at the back, like an exhaust system, creating enough power for forward thrust.

The first airliner to use the jet principle was the de Haviland Comet in 1949.

Concorde today flies at speeds which are in excess of 1600 kph (1000 mph).

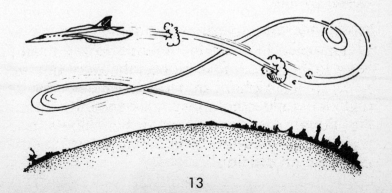

The Big Sucker

Englishman Hubert Booth designed the vacuum cleaner after he lay face down on the floor with a handkerchief over his mouth. When he sucked in hard through the piece of cloth, he discovered that dirt from the floor became trapped on the hankie, and this formed the basis for his invention.

However, the first cleaner he constructed was so large that it had to be transported by horses. Booth used to station the contraption *outside* houses, and suck the dirt from inside the building into the machine, by means of a long tube.

The Concrete Flowerpot Man

A French gardener called Joseph Monier came across the idea for rein-forced concrete while he was making flowerpots in his garden in 1849. He needed to use much larger flowerpots for his plants than were readi-ly available. So he decided to make them himself by covering wire netting with cement – the basic principle for reinforced concrete. Without his invention, we wouldn't have been able to build skyscrapers, dams or bridges.

Putting His Foot In It

A Yorkshireman, who repaired lawn mowers for a living, was so concerned at the number of accidents caused by rotary mowers that he was determined to do something about it. So Paul Adcock from Leeds, England, set about designing a safety blade for the machines in his garden workshop, using a man-made compound called polymer. Starting in 1982, it took him five years to perfect the world's first safety rotary blade. He demonstrated the effectiveness of the design at a garden fair in Germany by putting his foot in front of the spinning blade. He removed it, unscathed.

On The Cards

Have you ever played a game of 'Snap' or 'Poker', and wondered how playing cards came about?

They were created by Chinese women in the year 969 to relieve boredom.

The modern 52 card pack originally came from France and is now used throughout the world.

The Invisible Ray

If you have ever broken a leg, or an arm, or any bone in your body, the very first thing a doctor will do before he bandages it up is to send you along to the hospital to have the bone X-rayed. The X-ray will show how bad the break is.

X-rays are a means of taking photographs through the skin of the bones and organs beneath, and they have been vital in the medical world for nearly 100 years. Today, X-rays are not only used for diagnosing broken bones, but for most internal examinations as well. They are also used extensively in industry to search for stress fractures in steel or concrete.

Remarkably, the X-ray was discovered by accident in 1895. A German professor called William Konrad Rontgen was experimenting with vacuum tubes when he found that if he passed an electric current through the tube and on to a special piece of paper that had been treated with a substance called barium platinocyanide, the paper glowed even though there was a piece of cardboard in between. The effect continued even when he covered the tube with black cardboard, or took the paper into another room. He soon realised that the glow was caused by an invisible ray of energy with which he went on to experiment further. When he put his own hand between the ray and the treated paper, he discovered the perfect outline of the bone structure beneath his skin.

The House Of The Rising Sun

More and more houses today are being designed and built to use power harnessed from the sun's rays as a very cheap and effective form of heating and energy. Yet, solar power is not a new concept.

Hundreds of years before Christ was born, a Greek scholar and philosopher called Socrates came up with the same idea, and recommended that all new houses constructed should make use of the sun's powerful rays as an energy source.

Tin Foiled Again

If it hadn't been for an American inventor called Thomas Edison and a piece of silver foil, Michael Jackson and Madonna might never have sung on record. Indeed, we might never have had the music charts.

He was the man who discovered sound recording, from which came tape recorders, records and compact discs.

Edison designed and built a machine called a phonograph which could record and actually play back sounds. He made his early recordings by talking into a large horn. This was connected to a needle and placed over a cylinder covered in tin foil. A handle at one end of the device rotated the cylinder. As Edison shouted into the horn, the sound waves from his voice made the needle vibrate and scratch tiny marks into the tin foil. When the cylinder was wound back, the needle ran through the scratches on the tin foil and repeated what Edison had originally shouted. The sound waves were being sent back down the horn, which acted like a loudspeaker.

The first sound ever recorded was a scratchy version of 'Mary Had A Little Lamb'. Ninety-five years later, in 1972, Paul McCartney and his group Wings had a big hit with the song.

A Peach Of A Game!

Ever watched a player making a slam dunk at basketball? Well, when the game was first invented in 1891, that kind of shot would have been impossible to make. Dr James Naismith, a Canadian teacher, devised the game at the International Young Men's Christian Association School in Springfield, Massachusetts, USA, by attaching two peach baskets to the balcony either end of the school gymnasium. The idea was to score points by throwing the ball into these baskets. The trouble was, once a 'basket' had been scored, the only way to retrieve the ball to re-start the game was by climbing up a ladder and taking the ball out of the top of the peach basket. Then someone came up with the idea of cutting the bottoms off the baskets to allow the ball to drop through.

Hitching A Ride

When the first American Space Shuttle, *Enterprise*, was undergoing trials in 1977, it was carried into the air, piggy-back style, by a Boeing 747 aircraft. On several occasions, the Shuttle was launched into high altitude from the back of this converted airliner.

Wash And Brush Up

We might still be washing our clothes by hand if it hadn't been for an English upholsterer called Henry Sidgier. He designed the world's first washing machine in 1782.

Sidgier constructed a cylindrical cage made entirely of wooden rods, which he placed in a hexagonal tub and turned by means of a crank handle. There was one drawback, however, the machine had to be filled and emptied by hand, which took a long, long time.

It wasn't until 1906 that Alva Fisher from Chicago, USA, developed the first electrical powered washing tub.

The Biscuit Tin TV

In these days of global television when, at the press of a button, live pictures can be sent from the moon and outer space right into our living rooms in glorious colour, it is hard to imagine that John Logie Baird constructed the first TV out of ordinary household items and scraps. He used old biscuit tins, knitting needles, bicycle lamps, electric motors and parts from broken down radio sets. But on 2 October, 1925, he managed to transmit a picture of a ventriloquist's dummy from one room to another in his attic apartment in London, England.

Baird scanned his pictures with a cardboard disc containing a series of cut-out holes. He span the disc very fast on the point of a knitting needle. He shone light on to the revolving disc, which lit up different parts of the picture in a regular order and converted them into electric currents. These were then transmitted to a receiver, which converted them back into a picture.

Baird was so excited with the success of his first experiment that he rushed out into the street and grabbed a frightened 15 year-old boy named William Taynton. He set him down in front of the crude device, and switched on again. Thus, William Taynton became the first person ever to appear on television.

That'll Do Nicely

T he credit card was invented by an American oil company in 1920, for use when buying petrol. 30 years later, Diners Club Incorporated introduced a credit card that the public could use in hotels and shops.

Dry Up

I t had to happen.

The very first dishwasher was invented in 1899 by a Mrs Cockran from America. She simply filled a tub with dirty crockery and sprayed water on to it. However the drying up still had to be done afterwards!

Three Down, Four Across

T he father of the modern crossword was Arthur Wynne from England, whose very first word poser was published in the Sunday supplement of the *New York World* in 1913.

Steaming Into The Future

When the British engineer Richard Tre-vithick invented the first steam train in 1803 and George Stephenson introduced his locomotive, *The Rocket*, twenty-six years later, they had no way of looking into the future. They could never have known they were pioneers in a great discovery.

Since then, despite competition from roads and air travel, trains have continued to thrive and develop all over the world.

In France, the first aerotrain was invented using an experimental tracked air cushion vehicle, like a hovercraft, travelling along a single rail on a cushion of air. This was followed by the gas turbine train, capable of speeds of 300 kilometres an hour (180 mph).

In Britain, the train of the future could well be the 'Maglev', which is powered by magnetic levita-tion. Electric motors underneath the track create a magnetic force which lifts the train 10 milli-metres (½ inch) above the rails, and pushes it along. The Maglev is part of a shuttle service now in operation that connects the airport in Birmingham, England, with the railway terminal at the famous National Exhibition Centre.

La Mechanical Cow

Adrian Wareham from Christchurch in Dorset, England, became a dairy farmer with a difference in the autumn of 1987, when he invented the world's first mechanical cow. She was called Victoria. The cow was made of metal and designed with folding legs and all the mannerisms of a real animal. It was built out of rubbish and discarded parts from an old French Citröen car that Wareham found on the junk heap. It was also capable of travelling at 11.25 kph (7 mph) and made its debut in the great British Wine Transport Race from Sussex, England to Paris, France. There was, however, no truth in the rumour that the cow was invented to produce tinned milk!

A Fishy Forecast

American scientists have invented a way of forecasting the weather by using whales. Transmitters, which can be used for recording sea temperatures at great depths, have been attached to several species of whale, so that waters too deep or too cold for humans can be monitored easily.

Deep sea temperatures, which are very useful for predicting weather and wind patterns, are extremely difficult to measure in normal circumstances, particularly around the North and South Pole. However, whales are proving a great help to man. They can swim vast distances – from one climate to another – and dive to depths of over half a mile. Every time they surface, the temperature information they carry in their transmitters is beamed to an orbiting satellite and recorded.

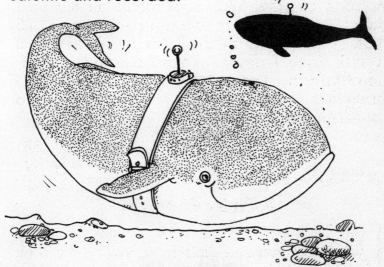

Blind Faith

The very first typewriter was invented by an Italian called Turri in order to help blind people to write more easily.

Run Robot Run

Robots have developed tremendously since they were first introduced into industry in 1962 by the Unimation Company in America. They were designed to simply pick up and transport objects from one location to another. Today, they can be used for a wide range of activities, which includes the building of cars and the detection of unexploded bombs.

However, robots are very slow and cumbersome machines. One thing a robot cannot do that a man can . . . is to *run*.

Scientists in America are working to rectify this situation. In Massachusetts, they have developed a four-legged, galloping robot, while in California, a six-legged bounder is in production.

A Roman Cover Up

The ancient Romans were the first people to design the bikini. A leather bikini made by the Romans and dating back to the first century AD was discovered in a well in London.

Skating To Disaster

The first pair of roller skates ever invented caused a disaster. A young Belgian musician called Joseph Merlin devised a crude pair of skates in London, England, in 1760. He wanted to impress his friends at a masked ball. The idea was for Merlin to make a spectacular entrance at the social event of the year, on a pair of wheeled skates whilst playing the violin. Trouble was, he had yet to invent a means of stopping. On arrival at the ball, he went skidding across the highly polished ballroom floor and crashed head first into a full length mirror, causing serious damage to the mirror, the violin and himself. It wasn't until 1863 that the American, James Plympton, introduced the more conventional four-wheeled skates we know today. The original idea was simply to provide a means for ice-skaters to practise when no ice was available.

Seeing By Sound

An invention that started life in the Second World War detecting enemy submarines is being used today to diagnose heart and liver diseases . . . as well as to monitor unborn babies in the womb.

Ultrasound was developed from the observation of bats. Bats locate objects in the dark at night by sending out a series of high-pitched squeaks, which in effect are sound waves. If there is an object in its flight path, the sound waves are bounced off this and sent back to the bat, who in turn builds up a picture of what lies ahead. Ultrasound works in virtually the same way.

Ian Donald, a doctor from Glasgow in Scotland, pioneered the use of this technique in the medical world in 1950. His aim was to study unborn babies by passing ultrasonic pulses through the mother's abdominal wall.

Tyred Out

Before Robert William Thompson created a basic form of pneumatic tyre in 1845, most wheels on bicycles and other vehicles were made of wood, steel or solid rubber, and that's how the name boneshaker was given to the bicycle. Thompson's tyre consisted of an airtight inner tube made of rubber and canvas, set inside an outer tube of leather.

Forty years later, John Boyd Dunlop, a Scottish vet, made the first rubber pneumatic tyre for his young son when he stuck pieces of garden hose pipe together with glue, and filled them up with air. He patented his idea in 1887 and formed his own company to manufacture them a year later. He sold his tyre firm in 1896 for £3 000 000 which today would be worth more than £98 000 000.

What A Cover Up

Wallpaper was invented in 1509 by an Englishman, from Beverley in Yorkshire, called Hugo Goes. He printed floral patterns from a wood block on to strips of paper, with which he covered the walls of his bedroom.

Elastic Power

Charles William Clark, from Maidenhead in England, had the brainwave of building a car that needed no engine to propel it, no fuel, and no batteries. He came up with an automobile that ran purely on elastic power.

The idea was simple. A giant elastic band was wound up inside the car on to a huge metal reel. Once the reel was released and the elastic started to unwind, the car was supposed to move forward. But the invention never caught on!

It's In The Bag

They do say that 'necessity is the mother of invention', and an American photographer called Joe Clark, HBSS, certainly proved it.

Joe, from Cumberland Gap, Tennessee – affectionately known as the Hill Billy Snap Shooter – worked for the American magazine *Life*, in the early 1940s. He managed to take the world's first underwater picture of a fish's eye view of fishermen, long before underwater cameras were perfected.

To get the shot he required, Joe simply wrapped his camera in a transparent plastic bag, found a shallow stream, and set the camera down on the river bed with the lens pointing upwards. He weighted the camera down with stones to stop it from floating away in the strong current, then he triggered the shutter by remote control. When the photograph was featured in the magazine shortly afterwards, it caused a sensation.

Getting It Taped

The first commercial video tape recorder, using a system called Betamax, was introduced by the Japanese electronic company, Sony, in 1975. It used cassette tapes, and allowed television viewers to watch one channel while recording a programme from another station at the same time.

A Special Brew

One of the most common phrases in Britain, a nation renowned for its tea drinking, must be: 'Let's have a nice cup of tea.' And it was a Briton called Large who designed the first ever electric kettle to help with tea making, in 1923. A copper element, housed at the bottom of a conventional kettle, was used to carry the electricity. Over thirty years later, in 1955, an automatic electric kettle, which turned itself off when the water was boiling, was devised by the Russell Hobbs Company.

Flopping To Success

When you are next watching athletics, take a look at the high jump and see the floppers in action. Modern athletes in this event use a special leap technique. They run towards the high jump apparatus and just before take off, swivel round, and flop over the bar on their backs. This method of high jumping was invented by a young American athlete called Dick Fosbury who introduced it at the 1968 Olympic Games in Mexico, where he won a Gold medal. The Fosbury Flop, as the technique is known, is now used by men and women high jumpers, and has taken over from such other 'jumps' as the *straddle* and *western roll*. It has been responsible for setting several world records.

The Eyes Have It

False eyelashes were invented in 1916 by an American film director, D. W. Griffith. He wanted to make actress Seena Owen's eyes appear to be much larger than they were in real life, for her role in his movie 'Intolerance'. Griffith believed larger eyelashes would give the effect he was after. A studio wig maker created the lashes to the director's design, by weaving human hair through gauze, which was then glued to Seena Owen's eyelids.

Going To The Wall

Nicholas Joseph Cugnot, a French Army officer, designed a steam-propelled tractor in 1769 to be used for carrying heavy guns. Unfortunately, a year later, a larger version of his tractor crashed into a wall in Paris, France, and Cugnot's name went down in history for causing the world's first motor accident.

Aspirin' to Greatness

An English clergyman called Edward Stone helped to create a concoction that has become probably the widest used of all headache cures – aspirin. In 1758, the reverend discovered that the crushed bark of the willow tree was a very effective remedy for relieving aches and pains. The chemical in the bark was called salicin, one of the basic ingredients of the tablet today, which was first introduced in medicine by a German called Dresser. Aspirin is a trade name used by the Bayer Drug Company in Germany who manufactured the tablets. The first bottle of aspirin went on sale in 1899.

At the outbreak of the First World War in 1914 when the Bayer Company stopped exporting their tablets throughout the world, a young Australian chemist called George Nicholas invented his own form of aspirins. He manufactured them as a 'Nicholas Product'. By taking the last two letters of Nicho*las*, and the first three letters of *Pro*duct, he came up with his own trade name for the tablets – *Aspro*.

Eye! Eye!

American scientists have developed disposable contact lenses that are designed to last for two weeks before being thrown away. In research, it has been proved that the lenses are far more convenient to use, and minimise the risk of eye infections caused by dirty lenses.

I'm Forever Blowing Bubbles

Next time you enjoy a cola or glass of sparkling lemonade, and the bubbles get up your nose, spare a thought for Joseph Priestly. He was the man who discovered the fizzy drink, in 1772. He lived in Leeds, England, next door to a brewery from where he was able to get plenty of carbon dioxide to use in his experiments with gasses. He used the carbon dioxide to make what he called carbonised water, the forerunner of fizzy drinks. Two years later, he discovered oxygen gas and called it dephlogisticated air! A real mouthful.

Upsetting The Filings

I f it hadn't been for an accident by a very clumsy cleaner working in a light bulb factory in Germany, we might never have discovered tungsten carbide. One of the hardest metal alloys, it is used for making drill tips.

During the First World War, there was a great shortage of industrial diamonds. They had been used for making light filaments, and German scientists were drastically trying to find a suitable replacement material. The scientists had been experimenting for several months in Berlin, and one night, an absent-minded cleaner upset a tray of iron filings all over one of the scientist's work. This caused a chemical reaction. The new compound hardened and formed the substance known as tungsten carbide.

Yabbaddabba-Doo! ! !

William Hanna and Joseph Barbera (along with Fred Quimby) invented the characters of Tom and Jerry during the 1930s and went on to produce over 100 cartoon movies for MGM.

In 1960, they created the first ever TV cartoon series for an adult audience, with the invention of 'The Flintstones'.

Peaceful Explosions

Alfred Nobel was a Swedish chemist and inventor. When he invented dynamite in 1867, he hoped that his discovery would bring about world peace. Nobel believed that dynamite, and gelignite which he invented eight years later, would be a powerful deterrent for warring nations. However, other people didn't share his views, and he was nicknamed 'Merchant of Death' for his inventions. This upset him greatly. He spent much of his later life working for the cause of world peace.

Nobel made a fortune from his inventions, and he used this as a foundation for the annual Nobel Peace Prize.

Phone Home

Without Alexander Graham Bell, E.T. would definitely *not* have been able to phone home.

Bell invented the telephone in 1876 by accident. At the time of his discovery, which dramatically changed the development of communications throughout the world, he was trying to design a new form of hearing aid for the deaf.

Although he didn't fully grasp the complexities of electricity, Bell devised a system of conveying speech over vast distances by the use of a transmitter and a receiver connected by an electrical conductor. He openly admitted on many occasions that he was quite baffled how someone in the USA could be heard clearly by someone in England, using his invention.

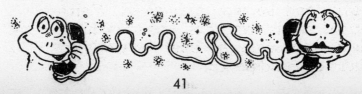

Catching The First Great Train Robbers

When the early railroads steamed across the American wild west, vast amounts of money and valuables were stolen from the trains by marauding bandits. Amongst them were Butch Cassidy and the Sundance Kid, and Jesse James. These were the first great train robbers. Trains were easy targets for hold ups, and outlaws often rode aboard, posing as passengers, until it was time to strike. In the early days, very few robbers were caught. It was a major headache for the railway companies, who came up with an ingenious invention to record on their tickets not only the names of each paying passenger, but their most striking characteristics, too! A series of punch holes itemised various descriptions such as age, height and colour of hair. If a train was then held up, the tickets of the passengers remaining on board could be matched up against those who had left the train, and accurate descriptions of the robbers could be given to the marshals. This system was the beginning of the electric computer and was developed by a man called Herman Hollerith, whose company was the forerunner of IBM.

Put A Zip In It

Whitcomb Judson was an American engineer who invented the zip, originally as a means of fastening boots and shoes. It consisted of a set of separate catches each with two interlocking faces, linked by chain, that could be pushed together by hand, or by the use of a moveable runner. Unfortunately it was not very effective, and Judson spent the next few years perfecting his design. Within four years, he had invented a machine capable of manufacturing zips, but instead of being linked together by chain, the fasteners were attached to a fabric tape. A year later, a Swedish designer called Gideon Sunback, who worked for the company making Judson's zips, devised a far more effective fastener using teeth drawn together by a slide, which is still used today.

A Talking Book

Raymond Kurzweil, an American science student, invented a machine in 1982 that could actually read books and magazines to blind people. Using a mini computer, the device can identify and scan-read most typefaces, before converting the printed word into speech through digitally stored sounds.

Faster Than A Speeding Bullet

Is it a bird? Is it a plane? Is it a rocket? No . . . it's Superman!

Superman, the world famous superhero, immortalised on celluloid by Christopher Reeve, was invented by two college students from Ohio, USA. In 1933, Jerome Siegel, a budding writer, and Joseph Shuster, a would-be cartoonist, devised their own do-it-yourself monthly magazine. In issue number three 'Science Fiction: The

Advance Guard of Future Civilization', the character of Superman began to take shape. Within a year, Siegel wrote the first Superman story, which Shuster drew. They hoped to sell it to a newspaper as a daily strip, but it was rejected by everyone they tried. It wasn't until 1938 that the superhero eventually made his debut in a commercial comic book in the first edition of Action Comics. Today, a copy of that first edition, which originally cost 10 cents, would fetch over 14 000 dollars.

Metal Claws!

Before an Englishman named Yates designed and constructed the first ever can-opener in 1855, tins of food had to be opened by hitting the top with a hammer and chisel. The blade of Yates' tin-opener design was similar to a crab or lobster claw.

Driven To Pottery

I n 1983, Japanese engineers invented a brand new car engine made entirely out of a revolutionary type of ceramic. The pottery engine is safer than a conventional one because it runs at a much higher temperature ... and reduces pollution.

Coming Down To Earth

A lthough he didn't invent it, Andre Jaques Garnerin did a tremendous amount to pioneer the development of the parachute during the 18th century.

Many of his ideas took shape while he was serving with the French Army. He was later imprisoned by the Austrians, and it was in jail that he set about designing and constructing a parachute which he hoped would help him escape. He aimed to 'fly' to freedom. However, before he could put his plans into action, he was released from jail.

Back in France, he made the very first parachute jump from a balloon 900 metres (3000 feet) over Monceau Park in Paris, in October 1797. His

canvas parachute was constructed like a canopy, and was 9 metres (30 feet) in diameter. The eccentric Frenchman descended in a tiny basket hung underneath.

A Spoonful Of Chocolate Helps The Medicine Go Down

When you have been ill, have you ever had to take horrible medicine that has left a bitter taste in your mouth?

Uuuuuuuurgh!

The best thing to get rid of the taste is a lump of sugar, or chunk of chocolate.

A woman from London, England, called Constance Honey tried to solve that nasty problem in 1937 when she produced a chocolate spoon. She only used this when giving bitter tasting medicine to children. The trouble was, the boys and girls liked it so much that they started taking far too much medicine than was good for them.

47

Getting The Point

T he safety pin, with its hidden point and coil spring, is one of the most ingenious inventions ever. It was the brainchild of an American, Walter Hunt, and its design has changed very little since 1849.

Reading In The Dark

C harles Barbier was a French Army officer who invented a system of writing which used dots and dashes punched on to cardboard to represent letters. He devised his unique alphabet while serving with Napoleon, to allow his soldiers to read the night orders by *touch* in the dark without using a torch. He called his invention 'night writing'.

Another Frenchman, Louis Braille who had been totally blind since the age of five, simplified Barbier's idea.

In 1834, he invented his own writing for the blind which he discovered after playing dominoes. Louis came up with the idea of basing his alphabet on the six dots of the domino, and

developed 63 different positions for these raised dots, to cover all the letters and punctuation marks. The dots were just the right size to be felt by the fingertips.

Braille later adapted his design for music, so blind people could learn to play an instrument.

In The Pink . . . The Red, The Yellow, Brown, Green, Blue and Black

T he game of snooker, which has become a multi-million-dollar sport in recent years, was invented in 1875 at Ootacamund in Southern India by British Army officers serving in the country. They had become bored playing billiards, and needed a new sporting challenge. The name 'snooker' was a term used to describe first year cadets at the Royal Military Academy in London, England.

If You Pass Go . . .

When the American stock market crashed in 1929, Charles Darrow, a heating engineer from Philadelphia, USA, found himself out of work. In his spare time, he started to invent toys and games which he hoped to sell. One night in 1930, he came up with a new game which was to change his life. On the kitchen table he sketched out a crude game-board, and drew in street names of his favourite holiday resort — Atlantic City — rather like a map. To make the board symmetrical, he added railway stations and utility companies. Next, he cut out a series of houses and hotels using scraps of wooden mouldings discarded by a nearby lumber yard, and typed out deed cards for the properties. With a dice, a counter and a wad of play money, he started the game, making up the rules as he went along.

The Darrows and their friends later spent many 'Monopoly' evenings together, playing the new game and using vast sums of toy money to buy and sell property. News of the game spread, and soon Darrow was manufacturing his own hand-made sets to sell. When the giant American games company, Parker Brothers, bought him out in 1935, demand for Monopoly was increasing. It made Darrow into a millionaire. By

1974 over 80 000 000 sets had been sold across the world. A year later, twice as much Monopoly money was printed in America than *real* money. Parker Brothers had originally rejected the game on the grounds that it was too complicated and lasted longer than 45 minutes.

A Little Sleep

Yoshiro Nakamata from Japan devised a revolutionary computerised chair in 1986. He claimed that anyone would be given the benefit of eight hours undisturbed sleep with only an hour's nap in his 'brain chair'. The hardest part about using the chair, however, was getting to sleep in the first place.

Gaining Support

An American debutante called Mary Phelps Jacob was in so much agony every time she wore a whalebone corset under her dress that she devised a simpler form of underwear for sheer comfort. One night in 1914, she designed the very first bra using two silk handkerchiefs stitched together with pink ribbon. She patented her invention under the name of Caresse Crosby.

Sweeping Up A Fortune

For many years, the word 'hoover' has been used to describe a vacuum cleaner, and it is now part of the English language. Yet, Hoover was not the name of the inventor.

An American janitor called Murray Spangler, who suffered from asthma, devised an electric sweeper when the rising dust from his broom started to badly affect his health. In June 1907, using wood, tin, a broom handle and a linen bag, he put together a device he called an

'electric suction broom'. Spangler took his invention to a relative, W H 'Boss' Hoover, whose own company manufactured saddles and riding equipment. Hoover liked the idea, made several modifications to the prototype, and started mass-producing the device in 1908, calling the contraption a 'hoover'.

Thunderbirds Are Go . . . On Rubbish

Many of the futuristic buildings and sci fi machinery that featured in the TV puppet series: *Thunderbirds, Captain Scarlet* and *Joe 90*, were made out of rubbish. Plastic and metal scraps, old spray cans and pen tops were among the everyday objects and pieces of junk the designers used to construct their minute film sets. Disused, painted string holders made chimney stacks that looked just like the real thing.

Happy Christmas

Every Christmas, it's a great ritual to send out greetings cards to your friends and relatives, and the card industry is a thriving business all over the world.

The Christmas card was first designed in 1843 by an Englishman called J C Horsley for his friend, Sir Henry Cole. The card, printed on stiff brown cardboard, depicted a sketch of a family eating, drinking and making merry. The words, 'A Merry Christmas And A Happy New Year To You', were printed underneath. 1000 were put on sale in London.

Americans had to wait 32 years before Christmas cards were introduced in the USA by Louis Prang of Boston, Massachusetts.

A Rusty Problem

Before the invention of stainless steel, knives, forks and spoons and most kitchen utensils made of untreated steel used to rust very easily. So after being washed up, they had to be very carefully dried. Steel is an alloy, and just prior to the outbreak of the First World War, Harry Brearley discovered that it attracted rust because of the carbon in it. He also found out that by increasing the amount of chromium in the alloy, and reducing the carbon content, steel became rust resistant . . . and thus stainless steel was created. Most cutlery today is manufactured to the Englishman's formula.

No Skool For A Genius

Thomas Edison, the man who was responsible for over 1000 inventions including the electric light and the microphone, had only three months of formal schooling when he was just eight years old . . . and then he ran away from school.

Cleaning Up

When Jean Baptiste-Jolly spilled a large quantity of a liquid fuel called camphene on to an overcoat in his home in Paris, France, he expected the garment to be ruined immediately.

Yet, instead of harming the fabric, the liquid *cleaned* it, and it was this discovery that led the Frenchman to invent dry-cleaning.

Baptiste-Jolly soon realised that by using a solvent instead of water for cleaning fabrics, the colour and the shape of the clothes were never affected.

He set up the world's first dry-cleaners in the French city in 1855.

Snap! Crackle! Pop!

Which is your favourite breakfast treat — cornflakes, porridge, or muesli?

Well, we have to thank an American lawyer for the introduction of the breakfast cereal nearly 100 years ago.

In 1892, Henry Perky, from Denver, Colorado, invented Shredded Wheat, and within years, eating habits changed all over the world.

Alexander Anderson got in on the act in 1902 when he developed Puffed Wheat, and four years later, William Kellogg produced the first Corn Flakes. Each year, nearly 100 million boxes of Corn Flakes are sold in the United Kingdom.

Stuck Up

I n 1928, Richard Drew, a research technician working for the Minnesota Mining and Manufacturing Corporation in America, produced the world's first sticky tape when he coated a strip of cellulose film with a rubber based glue. It was later sold on rolls and called 'Scotch Tape'. In 1937, George Gray and Colin Kininmouth introduced it to the United Kingdom as 'Sellotape'.

Trapping A Killer By Wire

When two Englishmen, William Fothergill Cooke and Charles Wheatstone, designed the first electric telegraph in 1837, little did they realise that eight years later, their invention would catch a murderer.

Cooke and Wheatstone's telegraph system worked by using five needles connected to five wires. When an electric current was sent through the wires, the needles vibrated and pointed to various letters marked out on a metal grid, allowing words to be formed and messages sent over long distances by electricity. They installed the system along the Great Western Railway to send messages along the line from Paddington, London. It was on the same railway line on 1 January 1845 that the device helped to trap a ruthless killer.

After committing a murder in Salthill, John Tawell escaped on the 7.42 London-bound train at Slough. He was spotted catching the train and a message was sent through the telegraph to London, notifying the police of his whereabouts and giving an accurate description of him. As the killer stepped from the train at Paddington, he was arrested by the police. He was subsequently tried and executed for his foul murder.

A Calculator As Large As A House

The very first fully electronic computer was built in 1946 by Americans J. Presper Eckert and John W. Mauchly, and was called ENIAC – Electronic Numerical Integrator and Calculator. It filled several large rooms, and contained over 18 000 valves, which often overheated and burnt out.

A Big Mac

Because there is so much rain in the United Kingdom, it was inevitable that a Briton would be the first person to come up with a waterproof overcoat to keep out the rain. That distinction went to a Scotsman in 1923 who was actually called Mackintosh. His first weatherproof coat was made by dissolving rubber into a substance called naptha, which he sandwiched between layers of cloth.

Caught On The Radio

I t was a German physicist called Heinrich Hertz who discovered radio waves in 1887. However, his discovery enabled a young Italian, Guglielmo Marconi, to invent a method of sending messages through the air over vast distances *without* using wires. This was in 1894, and the method was further developed into the 'wireless', or radio. In 1901, Marconi sent the first radio signals across the Atlantic between Cornwall in England and Newfoundland in Canada.

From his experiments, Marconi devised wireless telegraphy, which was quickly adopted by shipping throughout the world as a means of communication. However, the general public seemed strangely disinterested in Marconi's invention. It took a murder hunt to change it.

In 1910, wireless telegraphy was used in dramatic fashion to bring a criminal to justice.

Dr Hawley Harvey Crippen, wanted for the murder of his wife, was fleeing Britain for Canada aboard the SS *Montrose*, when he was recognised by the ship's captain. The captain sent a telegraph message back to England notifying Chief Inspector Dew, of Scotland Yard, who caught a faster boat to Canada and arrested Crippen as he disembarked in North America. He was later hanged for the crime he had committed.

Short Cut

Lawn mowers have come a long way since an Englishman called Plucknett invented the mechanical one in 1805. Before then, all grass had to be cut by scythe or shears. His design consisted of a circular blade which was rotated by two large wheels. Twenty-five years later Edwin Budding took the design a stage further. But it was not until 1902 that the world's first petrol-driven mower was invented — by the Ransomes Company of Ipswich, England.

Gene's Jeans

J eans were introduced to the world by an American sail-maker called Levi Strauss in 1874, who designed and made very hard-wearing trousers. The material used was a thick, twilled cotton cloth which came from Genoa in Italy. They were called 'gene fustian' meaning 'hard-wearing goods'. Somewhere along the line, the word 'gene' was changed to 'jeans'.

A Great Dane

I n recent years, Lego has become one of the most popular and successful toys all over the world. The multi-coloured plastic building bricks were devised in the 1930s as part of a whole range of toys by a Danish carpenter from Billund, Denmark. After Ole Kirk Christiansen was made redundant from his job, he had time on his hands, and used his skills as a carpenter to design a range of toys that were imaginative, educational and able to stand up to tough

handling from young children. He called these toys Lego, from the Danish words 'Leg Godt', meaning 'play well'. What he didn't realise was that in Latin, Lego means 'I am joining together'.

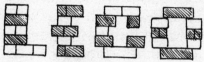

Comic Cuts

Comics and magazines have become collectors' items over the years, and today, famous first editions will fetch many hundreds of pounds on the open market.

The first comic was invented by an Englishman called Harrison, who lived in London. When he published the aptly titled 'Comick Magazine' on 1 April, 1796, he called it: 'The compleat library of mirth, humour, wit, gaiety and entertainment.' It led the way for such other famous comics to follow, such as *Beano, Dandy* and *The Magnet* in Britain, and *Captain Marvel, Batman* and *Spiderman* in the USA.

Turning Turtle

A very basic type of submarine was introduced as America's 'secret weapon' for sinking British ships in 1776 at the height of the War of Independence. It was called the Turtle and was designed by David Bushnell, from Connecticut, USA. The lemon-shaped craft was powered by two paddles which were operated by hand from inside, and a tiller which drove a rudder. It could take only one person at a time. Spring vents were opened to let water in to submerge the vessel, while hand pumps forced water out again to allow it to surface. For weapons, Turtle was fitted with two sharp screws at the front, controlled from inside by cranking handles. The idea was for the machine to manoeuvre underneath an enemy ship and then strike home with the screw into the bottom of the wooden hull. A waterproof bomb, with a clockwork timing device, could then be released into the hole, and primed to explode.

The Turtle never actually sank enemy ships. It had one unsuccessful mission in September 1776 and was then taken out of service.

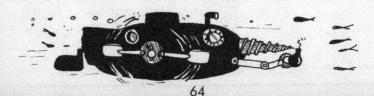

The Chewing Gum Trees

I t's no joke. When chewing gum was first concocted and patented in the USA in 1871, it really did grow on trees. It came from a sweet tasting gum called chicle, found in the sapodilla tree in Central America. Recently, though, synthetic substances have replaced it.

Dog Tired

O ne hundred years ago, a Frenchman called Huret invented a three-wheeled car that was powered entirely by dogs. The vehicle was driven by two large wheels at the back, with a single wheel in the centre at the front. Inside the rear wheels were placed tread-mills which the dogs turned in order to make the car move. Animal lovers throughout the country objected so strongly that Huret was forced to abandon his design.

Making Their Mark

I n an attempt to stop Army pensioners from drawing two or more pensions from the British Government in Hooghly, West Bengal, in India, in 1877, Sir William Herschel invented a system of identification using fingerprints. The idea was also used successfully by a local jail to prevent criminals from employing substitutes to serve their sentences for them.

Both Herschel and Sir Francis Galton discovered that no two people have the same fingerprints and that the patterns on each person's hands never change. They used this discovery to their advantage.

A Fingerprinting Department was first set up in London, England at Scotland Yard in 1901. The use of fingerprints as a major tool in the fight against crime was pioneered by Sir Edward Henry, who devised a way of cataloguing them.

Strike A Light

When the first friction matches were invented in 1833, they were known as Lucifers and were ignited by being drawn across a piece of sandpaper.

Keeping It In The Family

Siemens is one of the most famous family names in inventions. Ernst Werner von Siemens, who opened the very first telegraph factory in Germany in 1847, also designed the first electric train using a live electrical rail. He exhibited his invention at the Berlin Fair in 1879. Two years later, he launched the first electric tram which ran through the Berlin streets. With his brother, Karl, he established a number of telegraph factories all over Europe.

Two other brothers, Sir William Siemens and Friedrich Siemens, invented the open hearth method of making steel in 1861.

The First Walkman

The cassette tape recorder, which used an enclosed cassette instead of the more cumbersome reel-to-reel tape, was designed by scientists at the Philips Electrical Company in Holland. It made its debut on the market in 1963, and proved a popular forerunner to the 'walkman' system of today.

Sticking Together

It was during hunting expeditions into the mountains in the 1950s, that a Swiss inventor named De Mestral stumbled over an idea for a revolutionary new fastener, which he copied from nature. Throughout the trip, the inventor became increasingly more annoyed at

the way burrs from the burdock plant, commonly called sticky bobs, kept sticking to his clothing and to his dog's fur. He had great difficulty removing them. However, they gave him the inspiration to invent 'Velcro', a modern touch fastening used throughout the world. Although a trade name, Velcro is devised from two French words, velours (velvet) and crochet (hook). A strong bond is created when tiny hooked threads on one surface are pressed on to another, smoother, surface.

Cow Power

The waste products from animals have been used very effectively over the years to create fuel. Now, a plant in West Germany has experimented with cow manure. The dung is fermented in a series of huge vats until it decomposes. When this happens, it gives off methane gas which can be used as a fuel. The manure from 1000 cows can provide nearly 2273 litres (500 gallons) every day. Scientists are hoping that a similarly produced gas might eventually be used to fuel cars and buses, replacing horse power with cow power.

The Pepsi Generation

One of the most successful soft drinks in the world today is Pepsi-Cola, which is very nearly 100 years old. It was concocted by a man called Caleb Bradham, in his New York pharmacy. Caleb soon realised there was potential for selling a refreshing, thirst-quenching drink to the customers who used his drugstore as a meeting place. So he started to experiment with flavourings and colours before he came across his famous cola drink. It was originally known as 'Brad's Drink' although the name was changed in 1898 and registered as Pepsi-Cola. The formula Caleb invented has remained a closely guarded secret ever since.

How The West Was Fenced

The invention of barbed wire revolutionised America during the 1870s, particularly in the Wild West. At last the open plains could be fenced off cheaply, and cattle herds contained. In the past it had proved impossible to grow hedges over such a vast area, and wooden fences were difficult to maintain. Barbed wire solved these problems. It gave additional security to the settlers, too, when they staked their land claims. But some of the wealthy cattle barons who had been used to driving their herds across the country, showing no respect for other people's property, did not look too fondly on the invention. Some even ripped down fences or hired gunslingers to shoot anyone they found erecting barbed wire.

Several people claimed to have invented barbed wire, but Joseph Glidden, an American rancher, was the first man to develop a machine to mass-produce it, in 1873.

71

Green For Danger

When traffic lights were seen for the first time in London, England, in 1868, they were responsible for causing the death of a policeman. The lights, just red and green, and powered by gas, were erected 7.62 metres (25 feet) above the ground on a concrete pillar, close to the House of Commons. They were hand-operated by means of a lever. Within a month of their construction, the officer whose job it was to change the lights manually from red to green and back again, was killed when the gas exploded. These problems have since been sorted out, and traffic lights are used safely throughout the world.

In America, traffic lights did not go into operation until 1914. The first ones appeared in Cleveland, Ohio.

Antique Teeth

Believe it or not, false teeth were in use over 3000 years ago.

When rich or important people lost their own teeth through decay or in an accident, they actually bought real teeth from their servants or from peasants, who then had them removed. Sometimes slaves had their teeth taken out by force. These false teeth were then held in position in the mouth by wire. If two or more were needed, they were strung together by gold thread and inserted into the cavity.

In 1728, a Frenchman called Pierre Fauchard pioneered false teeth as we know them today, using crowns made from ivory. Another Frenchman, called Duchateau made the first set of dentures out of porcelain in 1770.

The Final Broadcast

When Guglielmo Marconi, the man who developed radio as we know it, died in Italy of a heart attack in 1937, the news of his death was announced to the world by his own invention . . . *radio*.

Lighting Up The Sky

Many of the world's musical supergroups – Queen, Genesis, Pink Floyd – have created their dynamic lighting effects on stage by the use of the laser – Light Amplification by Stimulated Emission of Radiation.

Since their discovery in 1960 by Theodore Maiman from the USA, lasers have been used for a whole range of different things – in industry, entertainment, medicine, micro-surgery, archaeology, astronomy, space research, warfare and defence.

Laser beams are made up of light waves of identical wavelengths. They do not spread out like ordinary light waves, so they are stronger and far more intense. They were first brought to the attention of millions of people in the 1964 James Bond movie, 'Goldfinger', when in one scene, the British secret agent, 007, was very nearly cut in half lengthwise by a laser beam. Although it was fantasy, the impact on the public was enormous.

Copycat

Ralph Wedgewood created carbon paper in 1860 for copying from one piece of paper to another. He coated thin paper with a solution of carbon mixed with oil, and left it to dry for several weeks. He then used a special pen, made from polished agate, to write on the paper. This made a perfect impression on the blank piece of paper underneath.

Roll Up! Roll Up!

George Eastman created the first roll of photographic film in 1885.

At first it was made of paper coated with a light-sensitive paint, then later from celluloid, and finally a cellulose acetate. The American inventor, who formed the Kodak Company, also devised the first camera to use wind-on film, and introduced the first camera, projector and film for home movies, in 1923.

Tanks For The Memory

When the first tank underwent trials in 1915, it was given the name 'Little Willie' to mislead enemy spies. It was powered by a Daimler engine and was capable of travelling at a speed of 3.22 kph (2 mph).

The second prototype tank, built shortly afterwards, was called 'Big Willie', although its name was later changed to 'Mother'. It had a top speed of 6.44 kph (4 mph) and carried a crew of six people, two cannons and two machine guns. When it went into service with the British Army, its name was changed to the 'Mark 1'. It saw action for the first time at the Somme in September 1916, and helped to bring the First World War to an end.

Number Please

T he automatic telephone exchange was created in 1889 by an American under-taker called Almon Brown Strowger after listening to town gossip. It was installed in La Porte, Indiana, USA, three years later.

Strowger, from Kansas City, had heard rumours that another local town mortician was paying the city switchboard girl operators *not* to connect his in-coming calls. In that way, he believed he was losing business, because would-be customers were being passed straight on to his rival. So in sheer desperation, he came up with the idea of an exchange that would do away with switchboard operators and allow callers to contact their own numbers by means of a push button system. This was later replaced by a dial . . . and later still replaced by a push-button system!

Pushing Its Weight Around

The Japanese are experimenting with a robot-controlled bulldozer which can be used underwater for tunnelling into the sea bed.

It is an ingenious device, far-removed from the more conventional bulldozer which was developed by an American called Benjamin Holt in 1923, when he decided to put caterpillar tracks on to a steam traction engine. He later added a blade at the front of the vehicle to enable it to move earth easily.

Fore!

The modern golf ball was designed and constructed in 1898 by Bertram Work from America. The ball was made out of a continuous rubber thread, wrapped around a soft core of rubber. The outer coat, now produced in synthetic plastic, was originally made of a substance called gutta-percha.

Before Work came along, golf balls were made by stuffing feathers tightly into a hand stitched leather case.

Pedal Power

On 12 June, 1979, a young American called Bryan Allen pedalled his way into the history books when he cycled across the English Channel . . . in a unique plane.

The Gossamer Albatross was remarkable because it had no engine to propel it. It was driven only by leg-power and a couple of bicycle pedals. The plane was the innovation of Paul MacCready, an aerodynamics engineer from California, USA. Two years before, he invented his first pedal plane 'Gossamer Condor', and in 1981 he introduced another, 'Solar Challenger', an aeroplane powered only by the sun. It had a top speed of 50 kph (31 mph).

Cashing Up

James Ritty, an American store owner from Dayton, Ohio, USA invented the cash register in order to stop his shop assistants pilfering the takings. It was based on the principle of a ship's log, which recorded the distance ships travel each day. The store-keeper came across the idea during a business trip by sea to Europe, and designed a machine that recorded every cent taken in his shop.

The device, introduced in 1879, consisted of a series of metal keys, specially marked out in dollars and cents. When money was taken from a customer, the keys corresponding to that amount were pressed down and the figure recorded by means of a flag which popped up into a dial at the top of the machine for everyone to see. At the same time, the sum of money was automatically printed on to a piece of paper.

Electric Socks

John Logie Baird, who pioneered television in Britain, patented several other of his designs, including thermostatic socks to keep feet warm in winter and cool in summer, which he sold in shops in Glasgow, Scotland. He also designed a safety razor that cut him, pneumatic soles for shoes which burst when they were walked on, and a machine for making imitation diamonds which blew up.

Getting The Bullet

Trains of the future are being developed to travel in special tunnels from which all the air has been removed to create a vacuum.

These vacuum bullet trains, powered by electromagnetism or gas turbines, will be able to reach incredibly fast speeds.

Getting The Bird

During harvest time in Britain, wood pigeons and other birds cause untold damage, destroying crops simply by eating the ripening wheat, barley or corn. The birds can eat at least their weight in grain every day. Unfortunately, conventional scarecrows have proved to be no deterrent against the marauders from the sky. But a British designer has come up with a novel way of solving the problem. He has invented a mechanical hawk, which, to a pigeon, looks very real indeed. The bird of prey sloops low, backwards and forwards across the crop fields, on an electric aerial runway. Its flight sequence along the 54-metre (180-foot) track is controlled by means of a micro-processor.

A Do-It-Yourself Puncture Kit

Changing a wheel on a car or fixing a flat tyre isn't one of the most pleasant jobs, especially at night, or in the pouring rain. However, in 1972 the Dunlop Company in England solved the problem with a tyre that mended itself after a puncture.

The safety tyre was constructed with a canister, containing a liquid sealing substance, built inside its wall. When the tyre was punctured and deflated, this action caused the canister to break open, releasing the liquid to seal the hole and mend the puncture. Heat then generated by the vaporizing sealer helped to reflate the tyre, allowing the car to be driven safely.

Blow It!

S ir Charles Wheatstone who, along with William Cooke designed the electric telegraph, was also a musical instrument maker. In 1829 he managed to invent both the mouth organ *and* the concertina.

The Red-Faced Doctor

A young French doctor called Rene Theodore Hyacinthe Laennec invented the stethoscope in 1816 to spare his blushes, after he was asked to examine a young woman he suspected of having a heart complaint. In the past, doctors examined their patients by placing their ear against the naked part of the body causing the trouble. On this particular day, Laennec was too shy to put his ear against the woman's naked chest to examine her, so he used a rolled up newspaper instead to listen to her heart. Later, in the park, he discovered some children playing with a fallen log. As one child tapped at the end of the tree trunk, his friend listened at the other end for the amplified sound. Using this same idea, the doctor constructed a wooden cylinder 25 centimetres (10 inches) long for use when examining patients.

Cut Price!

Michael Cullen revolutionized the way we shop in 1930, when he invented the supermarket and opened his first store at Jamaica, Long Island, New York, USA.

The interior of the store had no expensive fittings or decor, to keep costs down, and all the items displayed for sale were stacked up on the floor. Customers simply walked around the piles, picking up what they needed, and paid for the goods when they had finished shopping. It caught on in a big way!

Don't Look Down!

The American aviator Charles Lindbergh, who pioneered many innovations in early flying and became the first man to fly solo across the Atlantic in his plane, 'Spirit of St Louis' in 1927, was scared of heights.

Cat's Eye Catching

Driving to his house in Halifax, England one night in 1933, Percy Shaw came across a blanket of fog. This made it almost impossible for him to see where he was going. Suddenly, by the side of the road, his headlights picked out the bright reflection of a cat's eyes, penetrating the dense fog.

The incident gave Percy an idea of how he could light up the highway in the poorest visibility by using reflectors to show drivers exactly where the centre of the road was.

After months of experimenting, he came up with an ingenious answer, and named his design, 'cat's eyes'. He mounted two glass prisms into a rubber mould. These directed incoming light along its own path by means of a sealed aluminium mirror behind. There were two prisms in each mould, facing in opposite directions which reflected car headlights immediately. They were self-cleaning, too. Every time a vehicle passed over the device, the stud was depressed and the glass face pushed against a rubber pad, which cleaned the reflector.

Percy's own cat's eyes are now in use on every major road in Britain, and many more throughout the world.

Cooking Without Fire

T he microwave oven, developed by the American Raytheon Manufacturing Company in 1953, was the first original form of cooking since primitive man discovered how to make fire.

Under The Pole

T he US Naval Submarine, 'Nautilus', was the first craft of any kind to be nuclear-powered. It was launched in 1955 and in its first two years travelled 99 800 kilometres (62 000 miles) without refuelling. In 1958, it became the first submarine to travel under the North Pole.

Chocolate Bars From Outer Space?

The 'Mars bar' certainly *wasn't* a futuristic name thought up by an advertising agency to sell a chocolate bar to the public, although many people believe that is how the name evolved. In truth, the Mars bar takes its name from the very man who invented it during the 1920s, Forrest Mars. An American by birth, Forrest set up his company in England where the Mars bar made its debut. His father, Frank Clarence Mars, was a candy maker from Seattle, USA, who produced the first Milky Way chocolate bar in 1923.

Today, the Mars family is worth 5 billion dollars, and is one of the ten richest families in the world.

A Snake In The Works

The Odetics Company in California, USA, have created a 9-metre (30-feet)-long robot snake. It has been designed to service and maintain networks of pipes and tubing, like sewers, nuclear power stations, air conditioning systems and oil pipelines.

The snake, which can carry tools on its back, is built in half-metre (2-foot) sections with wheels on each side. The front end has been designed to operate like a mechanical robot arm.

Getting In A Right Cat Flap

One of Britain's most eccentric inventors was Arthur Pedrick from Selsey, Sussex, England. He invented over 200 different devices including golf balls with hinged air flaps to stop them spinning out of control, and a jet-propelled ship. He also designed an electronically controlled cat flap that only opened up for light-coloured pets, and kept out the darker ones. Arthur's own cat was ginger in colour.

Time For Tea

Frank Clarke, a gunsmith from Birmingham, England, was a very clever man who designed several ingenious contraptions. His most famous, in 1902, was a machine for waking him up in the morning with a freshly brewed cup of tea.

The automatic tea maker was activated by a revolving winder on an alarm clock. It worked a series of levers and springs, causing chain reactions. At a given time, a spring device was used to strike a match and light a small spirit stove where a kettle of water was placed. When the water boiled, another lever tipped the kettle up so that the water could be poured into a teapot positioned alongside. Minutes later, an alarm bell was sounded.

Serving On The Table

The Chinese have emerged as some of the best table tennis players in the world.

However, the game itself was not the brainchild of the Chinese, but of an Englishman, James

Gibb, in 1898. He called his game 'gossima' which was fortunately changed within a year to 'ping pong'.

This was derived from the sound of the ball hitting the bat and the table.

The first table tennis ball, which Gibb also created, was made from hollow celluloid.

Hanging About

In recent years, the exacting sport of hang gliding has become popular all over the world. There are even World Championships. But it is not a new sport, or a new idea.

Hang gliding was pioneered in 1891 by a German aviator called Otto Lilienthal who used the system to make a series of spectacular controlled flights . . . until 1896 that is, when he was killed in a flying accident.

In The Moog

These days it is possible to recreate the entire sound of a large orchestra by using just a single instrument, a synthesiser. Invented by an American, Dr Robert Moog, in 1965, a synthesiser is a machine that can reproduce the sounds of most other conventional instruments electronically. A whole range of signals can be produced by electronic oscillators which, after being amplified and filtered, are converted into sound waves. The sound waves are controlled by a conventional keyboard. Most recent synthesisers can be programmed to reproduce any number of different tones simultaneously. Others, called samplers, can convert any sound whatsoever – a gun shot, breaking glass, a toilet flushing – into a musical chord sequence. So it is possible to produce a record of a car door slamming and make it sound extremely musical.

It's Supercar

American car manufacturers, General Motors, unveiled the 'Sunraycer' car in the summer of 1987, to take part in the World Solar Challenge across a 3219 kilometre (2000 mile) course in Australia. The car, shaped like Superman's cloak, was run entirely by solar power and designed to create minimum drag. It contained an electric motor and a magnet, 10 times more powerful than a conventional one. Its top speed was 55 kph (34 mph).

A team of scientists at Cardiff University in Wales invented their own solar-powered car in 1986, which they claimed would go for 20 kilometres (12 miles) before needing a change of battery. The trouble was, there wasn't enough sun in Britain to start the car!

A Bag Of Compost

In a great effort to control pollution of all kinds, American scientists have designed a totally disposable plastic bag. Through a chemical reaction they have managed to bind corn starch to plastic, to produce something they call a *biodegradable* bag, which, over a period of time, erodes away into compost to enrich the soil. So . . . the rubbish tip could soon become a thing of the past.

Kidd's Stuff

The gyroscope works on the same principle as a spinning top . . . and remains upright at all times while rotating. A flywheel is set spinning about on an axis and remains on that axis. When the wheel is spun, its support may be turned in any direction, without altering the wheel's original plane of motion.

Gyroscopes have been used for many things, including compasses, gun sights, control mechanisms on guided missiles and stabilisers on ships. It was perfected by a German inventor called Bohnenberger in 1810, although a crude device had been developed by the British Navy in 1744.

In 1987, Sandy Kidd from Dundee in Scotland came up with the fantastic theory that gyroscopes could be used to achieve what scientists call 'space drive' — tremendous speeds from minimal energy. And he designed a machine to achieve this. It was 46 centimetres (18 inches) long with gyroscopes stationed at each end of a cross arm.

The device is a major breakthrough and can convert rotary motion into linear movement.

With the use of Kidd's contraption, it might be possible to fly to Australia in seconds, to the moon in hours, and to Jupiter in a matter of days.

Just The Parking Ticket

The parking meter was the brainchild of an American called Carlton Magee. It was first used in Oklahoma City, USA in 1935.

It's In The Can

Christopher Sydney Cockerell, an electronics engineer from Great Britain, discovered the idea for a hovercraft. An empty coffee tin, an empty can of cat food with the top and bottom cut off, and a hairdryer were the basic ingredients for his experiment.

Cockerell had a theory that ships could travel much faster in the water if wave resistance were eliminated. He determined that the best way to do this was to have a layer of air between the ship and the water. To prove his point, he fitted the empty cat food can inside the coffee tin. When the hairdryer jet was directed downwards into the space between the two containers, it was

discovered that the air pressure coming out of the bottom of the tins was far greater than that going in, (provided by the hairdryer). By squeezing the air through a narrow outlet, Cockerell realised that a heavy craft could be supported off the ground by a cushion of pressurised air. It was the principle on which the hovercraft was built in 1955.

The engine of a hovercraft consists of a large fan which forces air through slits underneath the craft to form a cushion. A flexible skirt made of strong fabric at the base of the machine retains the air.

The first hovercraft, 'SRN1', made its maiden voyage across the English Channel in July 1959.

Not Their Type

There is a fortune awaiting anyone who can invent an efficient typewriter that can be used in Japan. The Japanese language contains over 2000 characters which are impossible to cram on to a typewriter as we know it. So Japanese business people prefer to handwrite their letters instead. Typewriters do exist in the country, but they are slow and inefficient.

Recording A Disaster

I n a matter of years, it could become international maritime law that all ships must be fitted with a device known as a yellow cylinder – which is the shipping equivalent to the black box flight recorder used on all aircraft.

Developed by Lloyds Register of Shipping in London, England, the yellow cylinder would give an accurate reading of the state of all the relevant instruments on board a ship at the time of any sea disaster. Video technology would be used to compress on to tapes a vast amount of data, giving records of stress, rudder angle, draught and metal fatigue. From these readings it will be possible to find out exactly what caused the disaster.

The device, which is virtually indestructible, being waterproof, fireproof and explosionproof, is jettisoned automatically in case of any major emergency. The device sends radio signals to give its exact position for recovery.

A Corny Tale

Two Americans named Moore and Hascall invented the first combine harvester in 1836. One large machine could cut, reap and separate the crops, and bag the grain in a single process. It was drawn by horses. After this first machine, many different kinds of machines appeared across America over the next few years. Most of them were inefficient, however, and needed sometimes as many as *50 mules or horses* to pull them along. It was left to an Australian, Hugh McKay, to come up with the forerunner of the modern harvester in 1884.

Double Dutch

A Dutchman called Hans Lippershey patented the telescope in 1608. The same year, he designed the world's first binoculars, which consisted of a single telescope with two eyepieces.

The Sound Of Silence

I n 1933, Robert Watson-Watt, a Scottish professor, was asked if he could invent a death ray, using radio waves, which could shoot down enemy aircraft.

'It's impossible,' he said, 'but I think I can make a system using radio waves that will detect enemy aircraft before they reach our shores.'

It took him six months of experimenting before he came across 'radar' (*r*adio *d*etection *a*nd *r*anging). It was a simple idea. Powerful transmitters sent out a stream of radio waves at the rate of 1000 pulses a second. These shot through the air at a tremendous speed until they hit an object in their way. Then they were bounced back at the same speed to be collected in an aerial and relayed to a tracking station. Here, they produced a 'bleep' of light on a radar screen to show the position and distance of the object in question.

When the Second World War broke out in 1939, Britain had 40 radar stations and was the only country in the world to possess such a system. Today, radar is used for the navigation of aircraft and ships, and for tracking satellites in space.

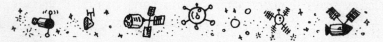

Stockings Made From Coal

The first truly man-made fibre ever invented was nylon in 1935. This was developed from a chemical made from coal. The man who made the discovery was an American chemist called Wallace Carothers. The first nylon stockings appeared in 1937.

What A Waste

In 1982, an East African company wasted over £50 000 000 on an enterprising system to turn molasses into motor car fuel. It failed miserably because the specially-designed plant was using more energy than it produced.

The Underground Farm

Most vegetables are grown *in* the ground ... but in a part of Northern Canada varieties of mushrooms, tomatoes and cucumbers are being grown *under*ground, over 1 kilometre (½ mile) below the surface.

Canadian scientists have developed the first subterranean farm, which went into operation in 1987. The farm has been built along miles of empty corridors in potash mines where natural geothermal energy – which comes from heat stored in the Earth's core – keeps the temperature at a constant 27 degrees Celcius (80°F), acting like a huge greenhouse. The great advantage is that in the very cold winters, most vegetables had to be imported. Now the Canadians grow their own, all year round.

A Right Pratt

Throughout history, inventors have produced a weird and wonderful range of disguises for hiding guns and pistols. Packets of cigarettes have been used, lighters, as well as umbrellas, shoes and pens. A knife was specially devised to house a gun barrel in the handle.

In 1917, an American from Vermont called Albert Bacon Pratt came up with the idea of mounting guns in Army pith helmets. To fire the device, the wearer simply blew into a long rubber tube that protruded from the top of the helmet and down the side of his face. Fortunately, the US Army declined Pratt's suggestions, for if the gun had actually worked, the terrific recoil would have broken the wearer's neck, or blown his head off!

Steaming Ahead

Pierre and Ernest Michaux were the first people to design and build a motorcycle in Paris, France, in 1868. Their machine was simply a bicycle with a small steam engine fixed between the saddle, which was connected to the back wheel by leather belts.

Getting The Fax Straight

I t is now possible to link two or more computers by telephone – and to send pictures and printed documents over the phone to anywhere in the world – using a facsimile machine, or 'Fax'. In a few years, it could make the sending of letters a thing of the past.

Money For Nothing

I n 1580 a Dutch engineer Pieter Morice created a water wheel which he set up underneath one of the many arches of London Bridge in England. This pumped fresh water to nearby houses. He could never have hoped, however, that over 400 years later his descendants would still be receiving money for his simple invention.

Morice and his family were granted a licence to use the arches at London Bridge for a period of 500 years. When the original bridge was replaced in the 1800s, the new structure had no suitable site to house the wheel, so the Dutchman's relatives were awarded compensation to be paid annually until the licence ran out . . . in the 21st Century. Each year, they receive nearly £4000 from the Thames Water Authority, and the contract still has just under 100 years to run.

Bang! Bang! Bang!

The rapid firing machine gun was the brainchild of an English lawyer called James Puckle in 1718. The single barrelled gun was fitted with a cylindrical magazine. This was turned by a crank handle to deliver bullets into the chamber. It could fire 9 bullets a minute.

Richard Gatling, an American planter from North Carolina, USA, designed a gun with ten barrels which revolved on an axle when turned by a handle. It was fed by a 240 bullet magazine and fired nearly 1000 bullets in 60 seconds.

Today, a modern machine gun can let off over 100 bullets every second.

Come On Down

An amazing computer toy developed in America is called 'Mr Gameshow', and it presents three different word games, each one with various skill levels. It comes complete with a small robot question master which can actually speak using a voice synthesiser and lip synchronisation. The robot has a vocabulary of 700 words, and if a player gets a question wrong, it unleashes a whole range of insults along with a shake of the head and shrug of the hands.

Flushed With Success

Lavatories have been in existence for over 4000 years, and archaeological discoveries have found that the Mesopotamians used a stone device similar to a potty.

The water closet (WC) with a flushing cistern was devised by an Englishman called Sir John Harington in 1589. Another Englishman, Alexander Cummings developed the modern lavatory in 1775. He introduced a system incorporating a pull up handle which opened a valve above the toilet bowl to release fresh water from a tank.

The handle simultaneously opened a valve in the side of the bowl to allow the contents to flow out into a cesspool. Thomas Crapper, however, invented a flushing apparatus that worked only when needed.

Getting The Picture

Police all over the world can now build up a very accurate picture of wanted criminals from eye witness descriptions, using a device called an identikit. It was developed in America in 1960 by Hugh Macdonald and consists of a series of transparent sheets on to which are drawn different shapes of faces, eyes, eyebrows, hair lines, mouths, noses, ears, chins and a wide range of other facial characteristics. These can be put together to present an overall picture of the wanted criminal or missing person.

A later innovation, photofit, uses the same principle, but with photographs instead of drawings. Both ideas come from an earlier system devised by Alphonse Bertillon in 1878.

Now Is The Ore

Thanks to a Canadian called Marrison, we can now all tell the time more accurately. He produced the very first quartz crystal clock as long ago as 1929. Quartz is a hard, glossy, yet colourless, rock mineral. When an electric charge is passed through the ore, it will vibrate at a constant frequency, acting very much like the swinging pendulum used in old-fashioned wall clocks. These vibrations are used to control the speed of an electric motor which drives the clock hands.

The Royal Observatory in London, England, has a quartz clock which is believed to be one of the most accurate in the world, and keeps almost perfect time. The BBC radio time signal is taken from it and the sixth 'pip' marks the exact time.

The very first wristwatch using the quartz crystal system was designed by the Japanese company, called Seiko.

A Flyaway Name

Sir James Matthew Barrie, the Scottish writer, invented the girl's name, Wendy, for a character in his book, 'Peter Pan' in 1904.

Frozen Solid

There really was a man called Birdseye, who indirectly had a hand in developing the frozen fish finger. His name was Clarence Birdseye, a fur trader and biologist, whose travels took him to the frozen wastes of Labrador, in the Arctic. It was here that he discovered that food left out in the freezing temperatures froze solidly in seconds, yet still tasted fresh when thawed out. His discovery became the basis of the frozen food industry to which he gave his name, and which has become a multi-million dollar concern. Birdseye founded his own company for freezing fish in 1926 in America at Gloucester, Massachusetts.

Sailing Into The Sun

The first known sailing ships, using a single mast and a solitary square sail, were developed by the Egyptians in 3000 BC. And sailing ships were used throughout the world right up to the advent of the new and faster steam ships in the 18th century.

However, now that the world's natural fuel supply of oil is running out fast, the Japanese in particular are pioneering ways of returning to sail power to propel their ships into the 21st century. Indeed, the first sail-assisted commercial vessel for over 50 years – 'Shin-Aitoku-Maru' – was launched in Japan in 1980.

These days, the Japanese are designing ships with sails made of solar panels instead of canvas rigging, to harness the sun's rays and use solar energy to propel them. It appears that sometimes we have to go back to go forward.

No Nick For Schick

An American called Jacob Schick was the first person to patent the electric razor in 1928, which he invented to stop people from nicking themselves when they shaved.

Electric Frog's Legs

A dead frog was instrumental in the development of electricity during the 18th century.

In his experiments, Luigi Galvani, an Italian scientist, discovered animal electricity. He found out that when he passed an electric current through a pair of frog's legs, it made them twitch violently, and he was able to demonstrate the connection that exists between electricity and muscle activity.

Experiments such as these led Galvani and his fellow Italian Alessandro Volta to develop, and subsequently create in 1800, the wet cell battery.

Shopping From An Armchair

Within just a few years, we will be able to go shopping without ever leaving home. All we will need is a computer, a telephone . . . and a shopping list. The order will be punched into the computer and sent down the telephone line to the selected shop where the items will be priced and the bill displayed on the monitor for our approval. Money will then be simultaneously debited from the customer's bank account or credit card.

At the end of the transaction, the goods will either be collected or delivered.

A system like this is already working on an experimental basis in America and France.

A Flying White Elephant

Howard Hughes, the American entrepreneur who was movie mogul, oil tycoon, industrialist, aviator and adventurer during a very colourful life, invented one of the biggest white elephants in aviation history.

In the early 1940s, in order to help the American Government's war effort, he designed a metal saving aircraft out of plywood which he hoped would carry over 700 passengers.

Called 'Spruce Goose', it was, in effect, a huge wooden seaplane and became one of the biggest aircraft ever flown with five engines on each wing. It took him five years to develop, cost the US tax payer over 18 000 000 dollars and only ever flew *once*, with Hughes at the controls. Then it barely got off the ground.

It never went into service, and has been kept in storage ever since.

Horses For Courses

The unit of measurement known as horse power, used to describe the power of an engine, was devised by the British engineer, James Watt, who found out that a strong horse could raise a 68-kilogram (150-lb) weight 1·2 metres (4 feet) in 1 second.

Ta, Mac

A Scottish engineer called John Loudan McAdam gave his name to tarmacadam for building roads, although he had nothing whatsoever to do with its invention. McAdam was actually responsible for developing another inexpensive technique for road making in 1823. It consisted of a dry stone surface of rocks, packed tightly together and covered with small crushed chippings. The surface was bound together by slag and gravel. It was raised in the middle and had gently sliding slopes, to allow for drainage.

An Englishman called Hooley came across tarmac several years after McAdam's death in 1836, when he stumbled across an upset barrel of bitumen. The tar-like contents had spilled out on to a surface of slag and dried hard to form a smooth, yet tough coating. He decided to call his discovery tarmacadam in honour of the Scottish road maker.

Someday My Prints Will Come

If the three year old daughter of Edwin Herbert Land hadn't been so impatient when waiting for photographs to be developed, then the polaroid camera might never have been invented. The little girl pestered her father so much, demanding to know when the pictures would be ready, that he decided to see if it might be possible to create a camera that produced instant photographs.

Land experimented with polarized light and, in 1937, he set up the Polaroid Company of America, which, amongst other things, developed polaroid sunglasses. But it took him another 10 years before he introduced his instant camera. It carried a combined film and paper cartridge, incorporating the processing chemicals to develop the picture inside the camera in a matter of moments.

During the 1970s, Land invented a cine camera that produced instant film.

A Revolutionary Bleep

Sputnik 1 became the first object to go into orbit around the Earth in October 1957. It was launched by the Soviet Union to commemorate the 40th Anniversary of the Russian Revolution, and sent out a radio bleep as it hurtled around the world at speeds in excess of 28 000 kph (17 500 mph).

Way Ahead Of Its Time

Charles Babbage from Devon in England designed the world's first computer as long ago as 1834, as a means of making calculations automatically without relying on a pen and a piece of paper. He called the contraption a 'difference engine'. It was a huge machine containing thousands of moving parts and rows of wheels which represented the digits in a five figure number. It was operated by a crank handle and programmed by punch cards. It cost over £23 000 to construct – a tremendous sum of money in those days.

Sadly, the project was abandoned because the machine was far too complicated to build, and Victorian engineers could not make the parts needed with sufficient precision. The technology of the time was just not sufficiently advanced enough for the task.

Yet, Babbage's ideas paved the way for many others to follow, and, after he died in 1871, his huge calculator was eventually constructed from the plans . . . and worked.

A Magical Musical Box

T he phrase 'juke box' was an expression used by Negro slaves in America to describe a road house, and it was later picked up and used as the name for a mechanical music box which Louis Glass invented in 1889. He set up the first coin-operated phonograph system in a saloon in San Francisco, USA.

The Car That Looks After Itself

Engineers working for the Ford Motor Company have designed a prototype for a car of the future called 'Eltec'. The car will in effect mend itself. Designed to incorporate an on-board computer, Eltec will be able to take into account its own ageing process and make electronic changes to its system to compensate for natural wear and tear. Experts predict that the new car, which is still under development, will have a lifespan of over 25 years. However, a human still has to drive it.

Wired For Sound

The tape recorder started life under the name of the 'Telegraphon'. It was developed by a Danish inventor called Valdemar Poulsen and put on display at the World Exhibition in Paris, France in 1900. The device used magnetic wire instead of tape, which passed between the poles of an electro magnet to reproduce the original sound.

Brolly Good Show

The umbrella was invented by the Chinese in the 11th Century BC, and was used as a symbol of rank and status.

Umbrellas were made from cane or sandalwood covered in leaves or feathers, and they were designed as sunshades. It wasn't until 1730 in Paris, France, that an umbrella was made from oilcloth, and designed to keep out the rain.

The modern covered steel frame rib, which allows the umbrella to be folded up tightly, was devised in 1874 by Samuel Fox of Sheffield, England. It was named the 'brolly'.

There Are Cars At The Bottom Of The Garden

Henry Ford, founder of the Ford Motor Company, and the man who introduced the first mass-produced car with his 'Model T', constructed his first car in the barn at the bottom of his garden in Michigan, USA, in 1896.

Pointing The Finger

An invention that can automatically identify fingerprints has been working very successfully for the Spanish police since 1987. The device, known as 'AFIS' is so fast that it can match up more than 50 000 prints in a second, and handle over 6 000 000 sets of fingerprints.

Underwater Breathing

Jacques-Yves Cousteau, the world famous oceanographer, underwater expert and scientist invented the aqualung for deep-sea diving in 1943. He later devised a way of using TV cameras underwater.

The Big Bore

French engineer Marc Isambard Brunel – father of Isambard Kingdom Brunel – designed the first tunnelling machine in 1818. This was used to construct the very first tunnel beneath the River Thames in London, England.

The tunnelling machine was built like a large rectangular box with an iron shield, open ends and projecting teeth. It was pushed through the ground by means of a screw jack. Wooden shutters at the front could be removed one at a time to allow men to work on the tunnel face, protected from the pressure of the earth and water above. As the device moved slowly forward, another team of workmen lined the walls with bricks from behind.

Brunel got the idea for his machine by watching a tiny animal called a mollusc. This insect-like creature lives on wood and spends much of its life boring into timbers, devouring the wood with its huge jaws. Brunel used the same principle for his tunneller.

The Thames tunnel, which connected Rotherhithe with Wapping, was officially opened in 1842, and is still in use today.

Doing Away With Cash

F our thousand years ago, in the Middle East, metal coins were used for the first time as money. Paper notes were invented by the Chinese just over 1000 years ago.

Today, however, we are heading for a society that needs no money. Transactions can be carried out by computers and credit cards.

In New Zealand, the Smart Card was introduced in 1987. It is virtually a computer in itself, all housed in a wafer-thin piece of plastic.

The card has a built-in microchip which contains all the details of the card holder's banking credentials, and an ability to communicate with the owner's bank account. It also provides a wide range of financial services and it can store information about every transaction that is carried out when in use.

It can't actually speak . . . but – you've guessed it – they're working on it!

Where There's Brass

James Nasmyth invented in 1839, a steamhammer for beating out large squares of metal that most definitely helped the development of steam locomotives and the ship-building industry in Great Britain. It all started when Nasmyth set up a brass foundry in his bedroom as a teenager.

Making Curtains From Glass

Fibreglass is a very versatile and adaptable material which is made from very fine threads of real glass. It was invented by an American called Edward Libbey in 1839, and has been used in the manufacturing of a wide range of products including boat and car bodies, carpets, heat insulation equipment, curtains and pole vault poles.

Pardon?

Such was the vanity of the Victorians in England, that many people tried to hide their deafness from others by inventing a weird array of hearing devices. Some were hidden in false beards, or hair-pieces. Ear trumpets were specially designed into high-backed chairs, while hollow listening tubes were fashioned into hats and walking sticks. It wasn't until 1901, however, that the electric hearing-aid was patented by an American called Hutchinson.

Robotburgers

First we had hamburgers ... then came cheeseburgers ... and in a few years' time, we will be able to buy robotburgers.

Don't worry, they won't be made out of metal, wire and transistors. But in an effort to make fast food even faster and to speed up the process of distribution to the customers, an American company in Wisconsin is experimenting with a machine that can cook and package hamburgers automatically.

They have developed a robot arm that places the burger on to a hot plate for grilling. Sensors detect when it has been cooked thoroughly and send a message by computer to a metal grab which lifts the burger off the heat, flips it over on to a toasted bun, and places it on to a moving conveyor belt.

At the moment, the company has not invented a system for filling the burgers with relish, so this still has to be done by the human hand. But the design is being worked on. The company is also developing a robot which will be able to take customers' orders over the counter, process them, and then bring the food to the table.

So it really does seem that poor old Ronald Macdonald's days are well and truly numbered.

Eating The Plates As Well

In 1987, Liangerh Chen, from Taiwan, became the first man to design and introduce edible crockery. Made from compressed rice, the cups, saucers and plates can be eaten after a meal instead of being washed up in the usual way . . . or, for that matter, eaten instead of the meal. The edible tableware was designed to be used as animal feed after use.

Scooting Around The Studios

Film moguls in several Hollywood studios are using motorised children's scooters to caddy the stars to and from the film lots these days.

Designed with a tiny engine on the back, and a top speed of 29 kph (18 mph), the scooters are cheap to run and exhilarating to ride.

Pop Goes The Toaster

T he pop-up toaster was the innovation of a mechanic from Stillwater, Minnesota, USA called Charles Strite. The very first electric toaster had been made by the General Electric Company of Schenectady in New York, USA in 1908, using a system of wires wrapped around mica strips. When electricity passed through the wires, they glowed red-hot and cooked the bread. But it proved an inefficient method because the machine only toasted one side of the bread at a time.

Strite, however, developed the idea further, and used a clockwork timer to turn off the electric power when the toast was ready, which in turn activated a metal spring underneath the bread, causing it to pop up.

Going Up In The World

Through his inventions with hoists in 1852 which enabled heavy machinery to be lifted several storeys high in factories, Elisha Otis indirectly helped to pioneer and encourage the building of skyscrapers across America. His experiments with elevators led his company to install the very first steam-driven passenger elevator in a New York store in 1857. This carried six people. By 1889, the Otis Company developed the first electric elevator, which was pulled by cables and driven by an electric motor.